Celebrating Our Faith

Reconciliation • Eucharist

Michael Carotta

Harcourt
Religion Publishers

Nihil Obstat
Rev. Richard L. Schaefer

Imprimatur
✠ Most Rev. Jerome Hanus OSB
Archdiocese of Dubuque
January 28, 2001
Feast of Saint Thomas Aquinas

The Ad Hoc Committee to Oversee the Use of the Catechism, National Conference of Catholic Bishops, has found this catechetical text, copyright 2002, to be in conformity with the *Catechism of the Catholic Church.*

The nihil obstat and imprimatur are official declarations that a book or pamphlet is free of doctrinal or moral error. No implication is contained therein that anyone who granted the nihil obstat and imprimatur agree with the contents, opinions, or statements expressed.

Our Mission

The primary mission of Harcourt Religion Publishers is to provide the Catholic and Christian educational markets with the highest quality catechetical print and media resources. The content of these resources reflects the best insights of current theology, methodology, and pedagogical research. The resources are practical and easy to use, designed to meet expressed market needs, and written to reflect the teachings of the Catholic Church.

Photography Credits
Cover: Stained-glass windows at Zimmerman Chapel, United Theological Seminary, Dayton, Ohio. Photography by Andy Snow Photographics.

Gene Plaisted/The Crosiers—17; **Digital Imaging Group**—12, 28, 36, 37, 53, 65, 66, 74, 83, 90, 98, 106, 114, 115, 127, 130, 140, 141, 142, 143, 144; **Jack Holtel**—29, 49, 64, 87, 111, 126, 144; **Image Bank**—Stephen Wilkes: 32; **Photo Edit**—Stephen McBrady: 12; Myrleen Ferguson: 13; David Young-Wolff: 70; **James L. Shaffer**—122; **Andy Snow Photographics**—13, 64, 66, 95, 99, 103, 119, 140; **Eric Snowbeck**—78; **Stock Boston**—Bob Doemmrick: 102; **Stock Market**—Ronnie Kaufman: 118; **Tony Stone Images**—Peter Poulides: 9; Myrleen Cate: 131; **SuperStock**—Lisette Lebon: 8. Special thanks to the parish communities at St. Charles Borromeo, Kettering; St. Paul's, Oakwood; and Holy Angels, Dayton, for cooperation with photography.

Ilustration Credits
Biblical Art: Chris Vallo/The Mazer Corporation: 10–11, 18–19, 26–27, 34–35, 42–43, 50–51, 72–73, 80–81, 88–89, 96–97, 104–105, 112–113, 120–121, 128–129; **Children's Art:** 14–15, 22–23, 30–31, 38–39, 46–47, 54–55, 76–77, 84–85, 92–93, 100–101, 108–109, 116–117, 124–125, 132–133 (prepared by Chelsea Arney, Lisol Arney, Kaley Bartosik, Hannah Berry, Noah Berry, Morgan Brickley, Brittany King, Cecily King, Jackie Malone, Katie Malone, Bob Ninneman, Claudia Ninneman, Erica Ninneman, Laura Grace Ninneman, Brittany Smith, Lauren Vallo, Ryan Vallo, and the art classes of Holy Angels School, Dayton)

Printed in the United States of America

ISBN 0-15-901135-3

10   9   8   7   6   5   4   3   2   1

Celebrating Our Faith

Reconciliation

Eucharist

Celebrating
Our Faith

Celebrating Reconciliation

**I will celebrate
the Sacrament of Reconciliation
for the first time**

on

_____

(date)

at

_____ .

(name of church)

**I ask my family, godparents,
teacher, classmates, friends,
and everyone in my parish community
to help me prepare for this celebration.**

_____

(signed)

**Here are the names of people who are helping me
prepare for Reconciliation.**

A Blessing for Beginnings

"The Lord is merciful! He is kind and patient, and his love never fails."

—Psalm 103:8

Leader: Today we gather to begin the journey toward
celebrating Reconciliation.
We are ready to learn from one another
and from our Church community.
And so we pray:
God our Father, show us your mercy and love.
Jesus, Son of God, deliver us from the power of sin.
Holy Spirit, help us grow in charity, justice,
and peace.

Reader: *Read Ephesians 2:4–10*
The word of the Lord.

All: **Thanks be to God.**

Leader: We ask God's blessing on our journey together.

All: **Holy Trinity, live in our hearts.**
Teach us to love and forgive.
Help us turn to you in true sorrow for sin,
and trust in your never-ending mercy.
We pray in the words that Jesus taught us.
(Pray the Lord's Prayer.)

Leader: May the Lord be with us, now and always.

All: **Amen!**

WE BELONG

Your Life

What words would you use to describe a really good group of friends?

_____

_____

What does it take to become part of a good group?

_____

_____

What's the difference between a good group and an average group?

_____

_____

Where do you belong?

The people with whom you share important times and with whom you feel at home are your **community.** Everyone needs to be a part of a community. You weren't made to live alone in the world.

Your family is a community and so is your group of friends. You belong to another important community, too: the **Catholic** Church.

Your Catholic community comes together to worship God at Mass. We celebrate the **sacraments** together and continue to learn about God.

As you probably know, your Catholic community is much bigger than the group of people you see at church on Sunday. The Church is a worldwide group. In fact the word *catholic* means "universal."

No matter where you go in the world, you can always go to Mass and recognize your membership in the Catholic community.

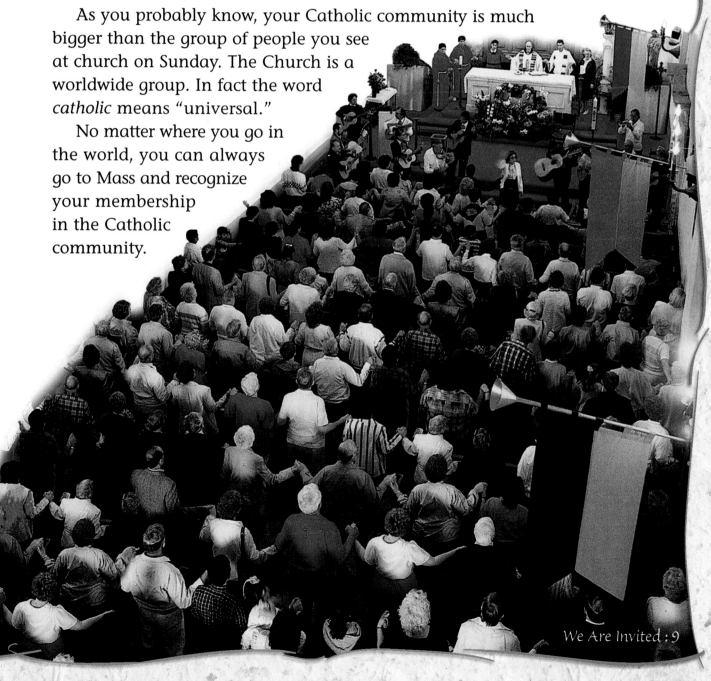

We Are God's Children

Saint Paul traveled to Greece to tell people about Jesus. The following tells of his words and actions in the city of Athens.

Then Paul stood up at the Areopagus and said: "You Athenians, I see that in every respect you are very religious. For as I walked around looking carefully at your shrines, I even discovered an altar inscribed, 'To an Unknown God.' What therefore you unknowingly worship, I proclaim to you.

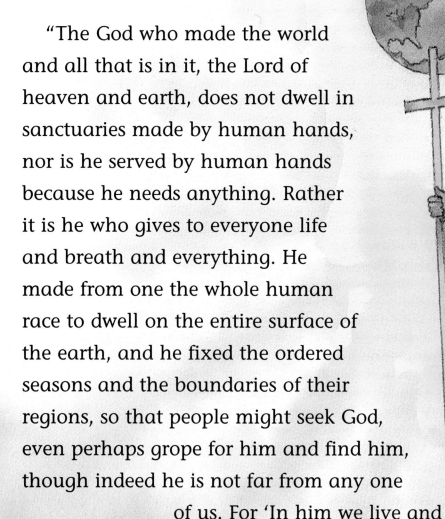

"The God who made the world and all that is in it, the Lord of heaven and earth, does not dwell in sanctuaries made by human hands, nor is he served by human hands because he needs anything. Rather it is he who gives to everyone life and breath and everything. He made from one the whole human race to dwell on the entire surface of the earth, and he fixed the ordered seasons and the boundaries of their regions, so that people might seek God, even perhaps grope for him and find him, though indeed he is not far from any one of us. For 'In him we live and move and have our being,' as even some of your poets have said, 'For we too are his offspring.' Since therefore we are the offspring of God, we ought not to think that the divinity is like an image fashioned from gold, silver, or stone by human art and imagination."

—Acts 17:22–29

We Remember : 11

Sacraments of Initiation

Like the people who listened to Saint Paul, we became members of the Church by being baptized. In the Sacrament of **Baptism**, we become part of the Body of Christ.

But there is more to becoming a member of the Catholic community than being baptized. Baptism is the first of three Sacraments of Initiation. The word **initiation** means "becoming a member."

You Ask

Why aren't the three Sacraments of Initiation always celebrated at the same time?

Early Christians were baptized, confirmed, and received into Eucharistic communion all at once. The same is true today for many adults and children of school age and for infants in the Eastern Rites of the Church. In the Latin Rite, Catholics baptized as infants usually receive First Communion around the age of seven and may celebrate Confirmation at that time or some time later. *(See Catechism, #1229–1233)*

Confirmation is another Sacrament of Initiation. In Confirmation we confirm our baptism, make a personal decision to live the Gospel, and receive the Holy Spirit in a special way. We are joined even more closely to the Church community.

The third Sacrament of Initiation is **Eucharist.** When we receive Jesus in Holy Communion for the first time, we celebrate our membership in the Church in a special way. Eucharist joins us completely with Jesus and with the Catholic community.

Living Your Faith

My Baptism

Fill in the blanks to record information about your being welcomed into the Catholic community.

I was baptized on

_____
(date)

at

_____
(name of church)

in

_____
(location of church)

My godparents are

_____

_____

List one or two ways you could remember and celebrate your baptismal day every year, thereby marking your membership into the universal Catholic community.

_____

_____

_____

_____

What's Important

Answer these three questions in light of what you've read in this chapter. This is important for you to know as you move toward the Sacrament of Reconciliation.

Who are you? (To answer this question, list words that describe you.)

_____

_____

_____

_____

Through the Sacraments of Initiation, to whom do you belong?

_____

_____

_____

Therefore, what's important for you to remember?

_____

_____

_____

Dear God—Father, Son, and Holy Spirit—you knew me before I was born. Thank you for calling me to be a part of the Catholic community. Help me always remain close to you and remember who I am and whose I am. Amen!

CHAPTER 2
WE CELEBRATE GOD'S LOVE

Your Life

Use an initial, a word, or a symbol to recall a time when a friend or family member really hurt your feelings—and, even if you've patched things up, it still hurts when you think about it.

_____

_____

What have you learned from this experience?

_____

_____

_____

Even in most loving families, people do not always act lovingly. Even best friends sometimes hurt each other. You know what it is like to do something wrong or hurt someone else. And you know what it is like to feel sorry and want to make up.

But we have a God who always gives us another chance.

It's a good thing when family members and friends forgive one another. When we **reconcile,** or come back together in peace, we heal some of our emotional pain.

When we **sin**, we do things that hurt our relationship with God and with others. We need a way to come back together in peace with God and with the Church. We want to say that we are sorry and that we desire to do better by trying to avoid sin in the future. We need to ask for forgiveness and to say that we want another chance.

God always loves us. God always offers us forgiveness and the grace to change our ways. When we desire to be forgiven, we celebrate God's mercy in the Sacrament of **Reconciliation**. We express our sorrow for our sins and accept God's forgiveness.

The Forgiving Father

Jesus told this story to explain the happiness that forgiveness brings.

Then he said, "A man had two sons, and the younger son said to his father, 'Father, give me the share of your estate that should come to me.' So the father divided the property between them. After a few days, the younger son collected all his belongings and set off to a distant country where he squandered his inheritance on a life of dissipation. When he had freely spent everything, a severe famine struck that country, and he found himself in dire need. So he hired himself out to one of the local citizens who sent him to his farm to tend the swine. And he longed to eat his fill of the pods on which the swine fed, but nobody gave him any. Coming to his senses he thought, 'How many of my father's hired workers have more than enough food to eat, but here am I, dying from hunger. I shall get up and go to my father and I shall say to him, "Father, I have sinned against heaven and against you. I no longer deserve to be called your son; treat me as you would treat one of your hired workers."'

"So he got up and went back to his father. While he was still a long way off, his father caught sight of him, and was filled with compassion. He ran to his son, embraced him and kissed him. His son said to him, 'Father, I have sinned against heaven and against you; I no longer deserve to be called your son.' But his father ordered his servants, 'Quickly bring the finest robe and put it on him; put a ring on his finger and sandals on his feet. Take the fattened calf and slaughter it. Then let us celebrate with a feast, because this son of mine was dead, and has come to life again; he was lost, and has been found.' Then the celebration began."

—Luke 15:11–24

Another Chance

Baptism frees us from sin, both **original sin** which we inherit from our first parents, and all personal sin. But because we are weakened from the effects of original sin, we are tempted to do what is wrong. Because we have **free will**, like the son in Jesus' story, we can choose to sin. The Sacrament of Reconciliation gives us a chance to ask God for forgiveness. It also gives us a chance to promise to do better.

Baptism, the first sacrament, is a once-in-a-lifetime sacrament. First Reconciliation is celebrated before First Communion. However, the Sacrament of Reconciliation can be celebrated at any time, again and again throughout our lives. Celebrating the Sacrament of Reconciliation is necessary in the case of serious sin. It is helpful even in the case of less serious sin. The good news is that when we are sorry and truly want to change, we are forgiven because we have a God who gives us another chance.

There are two main ways in which we celebrate Reconciliation. In **individual** celebrations, you (the **penitent**) meet with a priest in private. In **communal** celebrations groups of Catholics gather to pray and listen to readings from the Bible. Then each penitent speaks privately with a priest.

It's important to remember that whichever way we celebrate the sacrament, the priest acts in the name of Jesus, who brings us God's forgiving love. Like the father in Jesus' story, the priest welcomes us back home to our Catholic community.

Will God forgive you if you confess your sins in a private moment in your room before going to sleep? Yes, but it may not be as certain and clear as in the Sacrament of Reconciliation. Similarly, you could call up a friend and apologize for something and you might be pretty sure that your friend forgives you. But an apology and forgiveness in person is more certain and clear.

Even beyond that, Jesus desires that we receive the Sacrament of Reconciliation to seek forgiveness for sin and reconciliation with him and the Church. Ordinarily, this sacrament is the only way to have our mortal sins forgiven.

You Ask

What is the difference between mortal sin and venial sin?

Serious sin is called **mortal,** or "deadly." It cuts us off from God's grace and friendship. For sin to be mortal, it must be seriously wrong, we must know it is seriously wrong, and we must freely choose to do it anyway. **Venial** sin is less serious, but it still hurts our relationship with God and others. *(See Catechism, #1855–1857)*

Living Your Faith

No Grudges

The Bible tells us to hold no grudges. Use a symbol, initial, or word that indicates the person or feeling.

Someone who held a grudge against you for a long time.

_____

_____

How did you feel?

_____

_____

_____

Someone you are holding "a little" grudge against these days.

_____

_____

How does holding this grudge make you feel?

_____

_____

_____

What advice would God give you about holding grudges?

_____

_____

_____

_____

WELCOME HOME

A God Who Gives Us Another Chance

In this chapter, you have been reminded that you belong to
a God who always gives us another chance. Answer these two
questions as a way to reflect on getting or giving another chance.

With whom or concerning what do you wish you could have another
chance? What can you do to get one?

_____

_____

_____

_____

Who do you think wants another chance with you? What can you do
to give this person another chance?

_____

_____

_____

_____

Dear God—Father, Son, and Holy Spirit—you
are always ready to welcome me back. Help me
turn to you with love and faithfulness. Amen!

WE HEAR GOOD NEWS

Your Life

Which of the following would be really good news to you at this time?

____ One of your parents gets a raise at work.

____ You and your best friend(s) make the same team.

____ Someone you know who was very sick is improving.

____ One of your favorite relatives is coming to visit.

____ Weather conditions close school on Thursday and Friday.

____ You are the "student of the month."

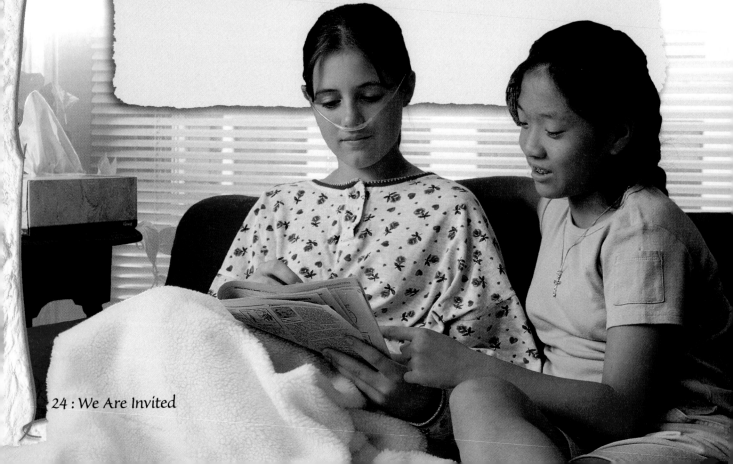

What's the best news you have ever heard? What do you do when you hear good news? Most people want to tell someone else right away. Good news is meant to be shared.

God has good news for us. God our Father sent his Son to bring us the good news of his love and forgiveness. We hear this good news whenever we hear or read the words of **Scripture**, God's word, found in the Bible.

God's good news in the Bible is especially important to share when we are feeling sorry for sin.

God's good news gives us the hope and courage we need to start again. Readings from the Bible are part of our celebration of the Sacrament of Reconciliation.

One Lost Sheep

People sometimes asked Jesus why he spent so much time with sinners. Shouldn't he be bringing the good news of God's love to holy people? Jesus answered them with a story.

"What man among you having a hundred sheep and losing one of them would not leave the ninety-nine in the desert and go after the lost one until he finds it? And when he does find it, he sets it on his shoulders with great joy and, upon his arrival home, he calls together his friends and neighbors and says to them, 'Rejoice with me because I have found my lost sheep.' I tell you, in just the same way there will be more joy in heaven over one sinner who repents than over ninety-nine righteous people who have no need of repentance."

—*Luke 15:4–7*

Words of Love and Mercy

Jesus' story about the lost sheep reminds us how much God loves us and wants to forgive us. This story and many others, can be found in the **Gospels**, the books of the Bible that tell about Jesus' life and teachings. The word **gospel** means "good news."

Readings from the Bible are part of the celebration of every sacrament. We call this the **Celebration of the Word of God.** These words of love and mercy help us see where we have sinned and how we can do better.

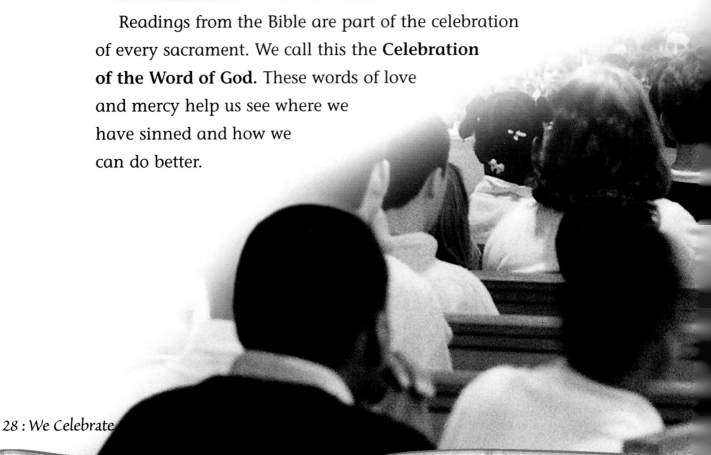

In a communal celebration of Reconciliation, we begin by singing a hymn. We pray that God will open our hearts so that we can ask forgiveness. Then we hear one or more readings from the Bible. The priest helps us understand what we have heard by sharing his thoughts about the reading.

When we celebrate Reconciliation individually, the priest may read or have us read a few words from the Bible when we first get together. The message of Scripture begins our celebration of God's forgiving love.

You Ask

How can we hear God speaking to us?

Scripture is God's own word. When we hear or read the Bible as part of the Sacrament of Reconciliation, we are hearing God's message for us. In a communal celebration of Reconciliation, the priest's **homily** helps us understand the readings and apply them to our lives. In an individual celebration the priest and the penitent may discuss the Scripture reading together. (See Catechism, #104, 1349)

Living Your Faith

Words to Live By

Which of these Bible verses has a special meaning of good news to you? Please explain below.

Psalm 23:1

Romans 8:38

Philippians 4:4

_____

_____

_____

_____

_____

_____

_____

_____

_____

_____

_____

_____

Good News

When a person is forgiven, it's good news to that person. Use an initial, a word, or a symbol to represent a person whom you need to forgive now. (It can be someone from your past or the present.)

_____

_____

_____

_____

_____

_____

_____

_____

_____

_____

_____

Dear God—Father, Son, and Holy Spirit—you give us the good news of your love. Help me understand your word and live by it. Amen!

CHAPTER 4

WE LOOK AT OUR LIVES

Your Life

Complete these sentences.

Things that make me happy are:

_____

_____

Happiness, for me, means:

_____

_____

I'm happiest when:

_____

_____

_____

_____

What makes you happy? Real happiness comes from sharing love, friendship, and good times. It may be hard to believe this, but God made each of us to be really happy forever. As children of God, we will be most happy when we are living the way God made us to live. That's the real truth.

God loves us so much. He gave us the **commandments**, or laws, as a sign of his love. The commandments show us how to live as God wants us to live. They tell us how to love God and others. Simply put, the commandments show us the way to real happiness. This truth gets lost in a society that seeks clothes, money, looks, power, and sex as the way to happiness.

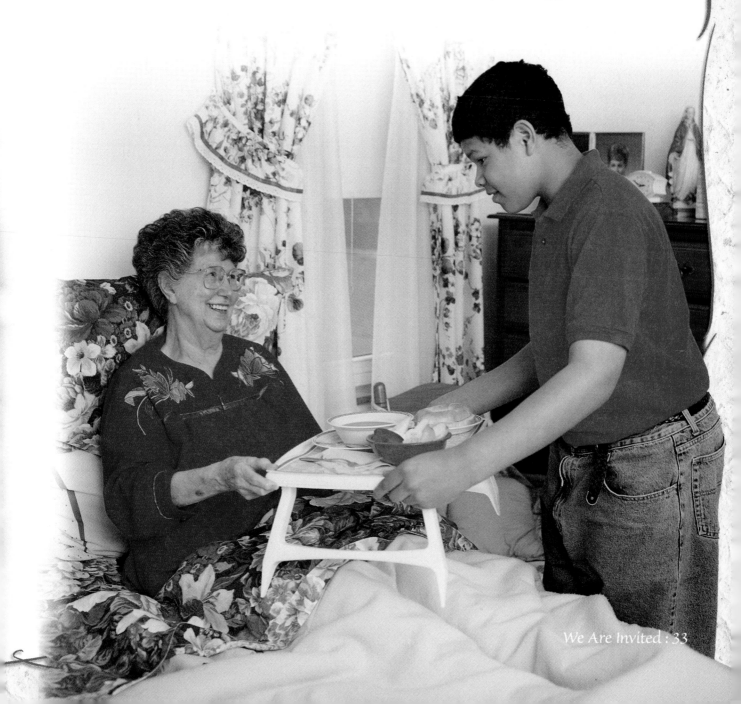

The Great Commandment

God made a **covenant**, a lasting promise of love, with the people of Israel. God gave their leader, Moses, the commandments as a sign of the covenant. The Ten Commandments were carved on stone tablets.

But the commandments were not just laws written on stone. The people kept these words in their hearts and they honored them in their lives.

The following event took place one day when Jesus was teaching in a small town.

"There was a scholar of the law who stood up to test him and said, 'Teacher, what must I do to inherit eternal life?' Jesus said to him, 'What is written in the law? How do you read it?' He said in reply, 'You shall love the Lord, your God, with all your heart, with all your being, with all your strength, and with all your mind, and your neighbor as yourself.' He replied to him, 'You have answered correctly; do this and you will live.'"

—*Luke 10:25–28*

How Do You Measure Up?

We know that we do not always live as God wants us to live. We do not always honor the commandments.

When you celebrate the Sacrament of Reconciliation, you look at your life and ask the Holy Spirit to help you see where you have made wrong choices. This prayerful way of looking at your life is called an **examination of conscience**. You measure your actions against the Ten Commandments, the Beatitudes, the life of Jesus, and the teachings of the Church.

Ask yourself if you are really happy. Ask, "What would Jesus say?" Are you really living as God wants you to live? How have you failed to show love for God and for others? Have you been selfish or hurtful? Asking yourself these questions will show you areas where you can improve your relationship with God and with others.

The Holy Spirit will not just help you see where you have gone wrong. God's loving Spirit will also show you how you can do better.

You Ask

What is conscience?

Conscience is the gift God gives us. Conscience is the judgment of our minds and hearts about whether our actions are good or evil. Conscience must be taught, or formed, to know the difference between right and wrong. The word of God and the teachings of the Church help us form our conscience. *(See Catechism, #1777, 1783)*

iving Your Faith

Who Is Happy with You?

1. Give yourself a rating from 1 to 10 for each of the following (1 = not at all, 10 = very much).

   How happy are your teachers with you these days? _____

   How happy are your parents with you these days? _____

   How happy is your brother or sister with you these days? _____

   How happy is God with you these days? _____

   How happy are your friends with you these days? _____

2. What behavior is keeping you from a better happiness ratio with someone listed above?

   _____

   _____

   _____

   _____

3. What behavior do you need to practice in order to obtain a better happiness ratio with someone listed above?

   _____

   _____

   _____

   _____

   _____

   _____

I

II

III

IV
V
VI
VII
VIII
IX
X

A Little Happiness

Who needs a little happiness these days?

_____ one of my parents

_____ a sister or brother

_____ a friend

_____ a neighbor

_____ a relative

_____ a teammate

Select one or two of the persons above and write down a specific action you can take to bring them a little happiness.

_____

_____

_____

_____

_____

_____

_____

Dear God—Father, Son, and Holy Spirit— you've given me the best reason to be happy: your love. Help me live our covenant of love. Amen!

Chapter 5
We Ask Forgiveness

Your Life

Use initials, words, or a symbol to complete the following statement:
A really poor decision I made that I wish I could change is

_____

_____

_____

_____

_____

_____

_____

Everyone makes mistakes. Everyone makes wrong choices at some time. But when you choose to do something you know is wrong, you sin. Sin is not the same thing as making a mistake. Nor is it always just a matter of feeling bad about ourselves or of making someone else feel bad, right now or sometime later. Others may never be aware of the effects our sins may have on them.

Sin hurts. It hurts you and it hurts others. Part of healing the hurt is taking **responsibility** for your actions. The Sacrament of Reconciliation gives you a way to admit that you did wrong, and it gives you a way to make things right with God's help.

In the sacrament you **confess**, or tell, your sins. You are given a **penance** to do. Accepting and doing your penance is a sign that you want to grow to be a loving person and want to repair the harm caused by sin.

The Man Who Changed His Life

The following is a story of a man who knew he was doing wrong and who wanted, with God's help, to make up for what he had done.

My name is Zacchaeus. My job is collecting taxes. I've never been very popular because no one likes to pay taxes. Also, I'm short, so people sometimes make fun of me. I used to make myself feel better by cheating people. I charged too much in taxes and kept the extra money for myself.

Then I heard about Jesus, the great teacher. He was very popular. Everybody wanted to see him. I heard he healed people and forgave sins.

One day Jesus came to our town. The crowds were so big I couldn't see, so I climbed a tree. You can imagine how surprised I was when Jesus stopped and looked straight up at me.

"Zacchaeus!" he said, smiling. "Come down! I want to eat lunch at your house today!"

"Me?" I said. "Nobody wants to eat with me!"

"That's right," the people grumbled. "We don't eat with sinners. This man cheats and steals!"

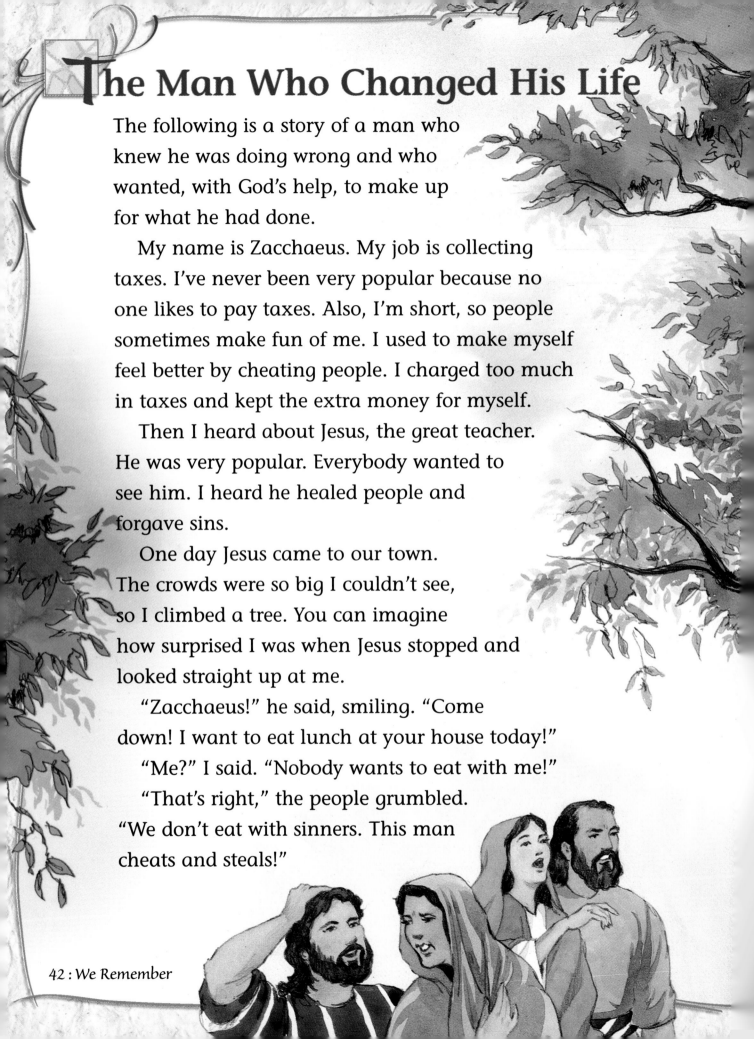

But Jesus just held out his hand. I nearly fell out of the tree. I led Jesus straight to my house. I fed him and his friends a big lunch. And then before I knew it, I was crying.

"I'm sorry," I told Jesus. "Those people were right. I am a sinner. I did cheat. I did steal. But I want to change my life. From this day on, with God's help, I will never cheat or steal. And I will give back four times the amount to everyone I've ever cheated."

Jesus gave me a hug. "Today," Jesus said, "God's forgiveness has come to this house!"

—based on Luke 19:1–10

Confession and Penance

Zacchaeus confessed his sins to Jesus. Then he tried to repair the harm for what he had done wrong.

In the Sacrament of Reconciliation, you follow this example. You confess your sins to the priest, who acts in the name of Jesus; then you talk with the priest about how, with the help of God, you can make things right.

The priest gives you a penance to do. The penance may be to spend some time praying. Or it may be an action connected to the sin, such as returning stolen property or helping repair something broken.

Doing penance helps you take responsibility for your actions and reminds you to think twice about how your choices for sin can and do hurt others. Penance is not punishment; it is a way to learn and grow to be more loving, while making up for one's sins. Penance is so important that our celebration of the Sacramentof Reconciliation is also called the **Rite of Penance.** Whether we celebrate Reconciliation individually or communally, normally confession and the giving of a penance take place privately between the penitent and the priest.

You Ask

Why do we confess our sins to a priest?

Confessing our sins verbally helps us take responsibility for our actions. God forgives sin, and the priest acts as God's minister by listening to our confession, giving us a penance, and encouraging us to avoid sin in the future. The priest is never permitted to tell anyone what he hears in confession. *(See Catechism, #1455–1456, 1467)*

Living Your Faith

Practice Penance

In the first column, draw or write about a wrong choice. In the second column, draw or write about something that will make things right with God's help.

Good Advice

Go back to the statement at the beginning of this chapter and review the situation you described. Based on what was discussed in this chapter, was your decision and the action to which it led a mistake or a sin? Now write down good advice you can give yourself in order to avoid repeating this kind of behavior.

_____

_____

_____

_____

_____

_____

_____

_____

_____

_____

Dear God—Father, Son, and Holy Spirit—you call me to make peace when I do wrong. Help me ask for forgiveness, do penance, and learn from my mistakes. Amen!

WE GO FORTH IN PARDON AND PEACE

Your Life

With an initial, word, or symbol, answer the following statements.
Recall a time when someone gave you a very sincere apology that helped reconcile things between you and that person.

_____

_____

Recall a time when you offered an apology—but you didn't do it as well as you wanted to.

_____

_____

Recall a time when you gave someone a good apology and it reconciled things between you and the other person.

_____

_____

Words, gestures, like a hug or a handshake, and sometimes tears are a sign that you are sorry.

In the Sacrament of Reconciliation, you show sorrow for sin by praying an **Act of Contrition.** In this prayer you tell God how sorry you are for having sinned and promise to do better and try to avoid sin in the future.

By praying the Act of Contrition, you are making the gesture that says, with God's grace, you want your wrong choices to be forgiven and want the chance to start over.

The priest gives you **absolution** after your Act of Contrition, in the name of God and the Church. You start fresh, with gratitude and hope, drawn and moved by grace to respond to the merciful love of God who loved us first.

The Forgiven Woman

The following is the story of a woman who told Jesus she was sorry. In return she received forgiveness, happiness, and love.

I knew everyone was looking at me. After all, I was known all over town as a terrible sinner. No one had invited me to this banquet at the house of Simon, a holy man.

But I had to see Jesus. I had to let him know that I wasn't a sinner anymore. I had been given the great gift of God's loving forgiveness.

I couldn't help it. As soon as I saw Jesus, I fell down before him. My tears washed the dust from his feet. My hair dried them. Then I poured sweet perfumed oil on his feet. The jar had cost me everything I had in the world, but it was worth it.

"I know what you're thinking, Simon," Jesus said to his shocked host. "How can I let this great sinner anywhere near me? But I can tell by her tears and her love that she has been forgiven."

"Yes, but . . ." Simon sputtered.

"Think of it this way," Jesus said. "What if two people owe you money—one a lot and one a little. You tell both of them they don't have to pay. Which one is going to be more grateful?"

Simon began to understand. "The person who has been forgiven more will be happier," he said.

"This woman has done more for me than you did," Jesus said. "That's how I know how much she has been forgiven."

Jesus looked at me with kindness. "Your sins are forgiven," he said. "Now go in peace." As I walked out of Simon's great hall with everyone's eyes on me, I held my head up. I felt like dancing.

—based on Luke 7:36–50

Contrition and Absolution

It's a mistake to think God automatically forgives people. Contrition, or sorrow for sin, is necessary for accepting God's forgiveness. There are many versions of the Act of Contrition, but each one says the same thing. We have sinned and we are sorry. We ask God's forgiveness and we promise to do better.

In a communal celebration of the sacrament, our prayer of contrition is followed by a **litany** spoken by the whole group. The Lord's Prayer always concludes the litany. In individual celebrations, the penitent prays an Act of Contrition after confessing and receiving penance.

The Sacrament of Reconciliation almost always includes private absolution of the penitent by the priest. Holding out his hand as a sign of the Holy Spirit's blessing, the priest prays, "Through the ministry of the Church, may God give you **pardon** and peace, and I absolve you from your sins in the name of the Father, and of the Son, and of the Holy Spirit." We answer, "Amen."

Our celebration almost always ends with a joyful song or prayer of thanks to God. Like the woman whom Jesus forgave, we express our gratitude for God's love and mercy. We are then encouraged to go forth in peace.

You Ask

What does the Sacrament of Reconciliation do for us?

The Sacrament of Reconciliation does exactly what its name describes. Through sacramental confession and absolution, we are **reconciled,** or brought back closer to God.

The Sacrament of Reconciliation has other effects. We are reconciled with our own conscience, allowing us to feel inner peace. We are reconciled with others, especially those whom we have hurt. We are reconciled with the Christian community, making the whole Church stronger. And we are reconciled with all God's creation.
(See Catechism, #1469)

Living Your Faith

I Promise to Do Better

Create your own Act of Contrition, which you can say anytime, regarding any sin. Then give your Act of Contrition a title in order to make it your own prayer.

_____

_____

_____

_____

_____

_____

_____

_____

_____

_____

_____

_____

_____

Letting Go

Because of God's love found in the Sacrament
of Reconciliation and found also in friends who forgive,
you don't have to hold on to something you've done wrong in
the past. Use an initial or word to signify something of which you
want to let go. Use an initial or word to signify something new that
will help you move forward.

_____

_____

_____

_____

_____

_____

_____

_____

_____

_____

Dear God—Father, Son, and Holy Spirit—
you free me from sin when I repent. Help me
accept your forgiveness and grow in peace
and love. Amen.

Catholic Prayers

The Sign of the Cross

In the name of the Father,
and of the Son,
and of the Holy Spirit.
Amen.

The Lord's Prayer

Our Father, who art in heaven,
hallowed be thy name;
thy kingdom come;
thy will be done on earth as it is in heaven.
Give us this day our daily bread;
and forgive us our trespasses
as we forgive those who trespass against us;
and lead us not into temptation,
but deliver us from evil.
Amen.

Hail Mary

Hail, Mary, full of grace,
the Lord is with you!
Blessed are you among women,
and blessed is the fruit of your womb, Jesus.
Holy Mary, Mother of God,
pray for us sinners,
now and at the hour of our death.
Amen.

Glory to the Father (Doxology)

Glory to the Father,
and to the Son,
and to the Holy Spirit,
as it was in the beginning,
is now, and will be for ever.
Amen.

I Confess (Confiteor)

I confess to almighty God,
and to you, my brothers and sisters,
that I have sinned through my own fault
in my thoughts and in my words,
in what I have done,
and in what I have failed to do;
and I ask blessed Mary, ever virgin,
all the angels and saints,
and you, my brothers and sisters,
to pray for me to the Lord our God.

Act of Contrition

My God,
I am sorry for my sins with all my heart.
In choosing to do wrong
and failing to do good,
I have sinned against you
whom I should love above all things.
I firmly intend, with your help,
to do penance,
to sin no more,
and to avoid whatever leads me to sin.
Our Savior Jesus Christ
suffered and died for us.
In his name, my God, have mercy.

The Jesus Prayer

Lord Jesus, Son of God,
have mercy on me, a sinner.
Amen.

Our Moral Guide

The Great Commandment

"You shall love the Lord your God with all your heart, with all your soul, with all your strength, and with all your mind; and your neighbor as yourself."

—*Luke 10:27*

The Beatitudes

"Blessed are the poor in spirit,
   for theirs is the kingdom of heaven.
Blessed are they who mourn,
   for they will be comforted.
Blessed are the meek,
   for they will inherit the land.
Blessed are they who hunger and thirst
for righteousness,
   for they will be satisfied.
Blessed are the merciful,
   for they will be shown mercy.
Blessed are the clean of heart,
   for they will see God.
Blessed are the peacemakers,
   for they will be called children of God.
Blessed are they who are persecuted for the sake of righteousness,
   for theirs is the kingdom of heaven."

—*Matthew 5:3–10*

The Ten Commandments

1. **I am the Lord your God. You shall not have strange gods before me.**
   Put God first in your life before all things.

2. **You shall not take the name of the Lord your God in vain.**
   Respect God's name and holy things. Do not use bad language.

3. **Remember to keep holy the Lord's day.**
   Take part in the Mass on Sundays and holy days.
   Avoid unnecessary work on these days.

4. **Honor your father and your mother.**
   Obey and show respect to parents and others who are responsible for you.

5. **You shall not kill.**
   Do not hurt yourself or others. Take care of all life.

6. **You shall not commit adultery.**
   Show respect for marriage and family life.
   Respect your body and the bodies of others.

7. **You shall not steal.**
   Respect creation and the things that belong to others.
   Do not cheat.

8. **You shall not bear false witness against your neighbor.**
   Tell the truth. Do not gossip.

9. **You shall not covet your neighbor's wife.**
   Be faithful to family members and friends. Do not be jealous.

10. **You shall not covet your neighbor's goods.**
    Share what you have. Do not envy what other people have.
    Do not be greedy.

Precepts of the Church

1. Take part in the Mass on Sundays and holy days. Keep these days holy, and avoid unnecessary work.
2. Celebrate the Sacrament of Reconciliation at least once a year if there is serious sin.
3. Receive Holy Communion at least once a year during Easter time.
4. Fast and abstain on days of penance.
5. Give your time, gifts, and money to support the Church.

Works of Mercy

Corporal (for the body)

Feed the hungry.

Give drink to the thirsty.

Clothe the naked.

Shelter the homeless.

Visit the sick.

Visit the imprisoned.

Bury the dead.

Spiritual (for the spirit)

Warn the sinner.

Teach the ignorant.

Counsel the doubtful.

Comfort the sorrowful.

Bear wrongs patiently.

Forgive injuries.

Pray for the living and the dead.

Examination of Conscience

1. Look at your life. Compare your actions and choices with the Beatitudes, the Ten Commandments, the Great Commandment, and the precepts of the Church.

2. Ask yourself:
   - When have I not done what God wants me to do?
   - Whom have I hurt?
   - What have I done that I knew was wrong?
   - What have I not done that I should have done?
   - Are there serious sins I did not mention the last time I confessed?
   - Have I done penance? Have I tried as hard as I could with God's help to make up for past sins?
   - Have I changed my bad habits?
   - Am I sincerely sorry for all my sins?

3. In addition to confessing your sins, you may want to talk to the priest about one or more of the above questions.

4. Pray for the help of the Holy Spirit to change and start over.

Celebrating the Sacrament of Reconciliation

The Communal Rite of Reconciliation

- Before celebrating the Sacrament of Reconciliation, take time to examine your conscience. Pray for the help of the Holy Spirit.

1. **Introductory Rites**
   Join in singing the opening hymn. The priest will greet the assembly and lead you in the opening prayer.

2. **Reading from Scripture**
   Listen to the word of God. There may be more than one reading, with a hymn or psalm in between. The last reading will be from one of the Gospels.

3. **Homily**
   Listen as the priest, by sharing his thoughts, helps you understand the meaning of the Scriptures.

4. **Examination of Conscience with Litany of Contrition and the Lord's Prayer**
   After the homily there will be a time of silence. The priest may lead the assembly in an examination of conscience. This is followed by the prayer of confession and the litany or song. Then all pray together the Lord's Prayer.

5. **Individual Confession, Giving of Penance, and Absolution**
   While you wait your turn to talk with the priest, you may pray quietly or join in singing. When it is your turn, confess your sins to the priest. He will talk to you about how to improve and give you a penance. Then, in the name of Jesus and the Church, he will give you absolution.

6. **Closing Rite**
   After everyone has confessed individually, join in singing or praying a song or litany of thanksgiving. The priest will lead the closing prayer and bless the assembly. Then the priest or deacon will dismiss the assembly.

- After celebrating the sacrament, carry out your penance as soon as possible.

The Individual Rite of Reconciliation

- Before celebrating the Sacrament of Reconciliation, take time to examine your conscience. Pray for the help of the Holy Spirit.
- Wait for your turn to enter the Reconciliation room.
- You may choose to meet with the priest face-to-face or to be separated from the priest by a screen.

1. **Welcome**
   The priest will welcome you and invite you to pray the Sign of the Cross.

2. **Reading from Scripture**
   The priest may read or recite a passage from the Bible. You may be invited by the priest to read the Scripture yourself.

3. **Confession of Sins and Giving of Penance**
   Tell your sins to the priest. The priest will talk with you about how to do better. Then he will give you a penance.

4. **Act of Contrition**
   Pray an Act of Contrition.

5. **Absolution**
   The priest will hold his hand over your head and pray the prayer of absolution. As he says the final words, he will make the Sign of the Cross.

6. **Closing Prayer**
   The priest will pray, "Give thanks to the Lord, for he is good." You answer, "His mercy endures for ever." Then the priest will dismiss you.

- After celebrating the sacrament, carry out your penance as soon as possible.

Illustrated Glossary for Reconciliation

absolution

(ab•sə•'lü•shən): The forgiveness of sin we receive from God through the Church in the Sacrament of Reconciliation. The word *absolve* means "to wash away."

communal celebration

(kə•'myü•nl se•lə•'brā•shən): One form of celebrating the Sacrament of Reconciliation. In a communal celebration the assembly gathers to pray and hear God's word. Each penitent then confesses, receives a penance, and is absolved privately.

confession

(kən•'fe•shən): Telling our sins to a priest in the Sacrament of Reconciliation. What we confess to the priest is private.

contrition

(kən•'tri•shən): Sorrow for sins and a willingness to do better (a firm purpose of amendment). Contrition is our first step toward forgiveness. As part of the Sacrament of Reconciliation, we pray an **Act**, or Prayer, **of Contrition** ('akt 'əv kən•'tri•shən).

examination of conscience

(ig•za•mə•'nā•shən 'əv 'kän(t)•shən(t)s): A prayerful way of looking at our lives in light of the Ten Commandments, the Beatitudes, the life of Jesus, and the teachings of the Church.

individual celebration

(in•də•'vij•wəl se•la•'brā•shən): One form of celebrating the Sacrament of Reconciliation. In an individual celebration the penitent meets with the priest in private. The penitent then confesses, receives a penance, and is absolved privately.

penance

('pe•nən(t)s): Prayers and actions done with God's help to repair the harm our sins have caused. In the Sacrament of Reconciliation, the priest gives us a penance to do. The celebration of the Sacrament of Reconciliation is called the **Rite of Penance** ('rīt 'əv 'pe•nən(t)s).

penitent

('pe•nə•tənt): The person who confesses his or her sins to the priest in the Sacrament of Reconciliation.

priest

('prēst): A man who is ordained to serve God and the Church by celebrating the sacraments, preaching, and presiding at Mass. The priest is the **confessor** (kən•'fe•sər), or minister of the Sacrament of Reconciliation. For the Sacrament of Reconciliation, the priest wears a stole. The **stole** ('stōl) is a sign of the priest's obedience to God and of his priestly authority.

R

Reconciliation room

(re•kən•si•lē•'ā•shən 'rüm): A room or chapel in which the confessor hears the penitent's confession of sins. The room is usually furnished with chairs, a kneeler, a table for the Bible and candle, and a screen that can be used as a divider between the priest and the penitent.

S

Scripture

('skrip(t)•shər): The word of God contained in the Bible. The word *scripture* means "holy writing." Scripture is used for reflecting on God's love and forgiveness in the Sacrament of Reconciliation. Scripture is proclaimed by a **lector** ('lek•tər), or reader, at Mass or in other liturgical celebrations. The Gospel is proclaimed by a deacon or priest.

sin

('sin): The choice to disobey God. Sin can be serious **(mortal)** ('mȯr•təl) or less serious **(venial)** ('və•hē•əl). Sin is a deliberate choice, not a mistake or an accident. We accept God's loving forgiveness for our sins when we show by our sorrow and firm purpose of amendment that we are willing to do better.

Celebrating
Our Faith

Celebrating Communion

I will receive
Holy Communion
for the first time
during the celebration of the Eucharist
on

_____

(date)

at

_____.

(name of church)

I ask my family, godparents,
teacher, classmates, friends,
and everyone in my parish community
to help me prepare for this celebration.

_____

(signed)

Here are the names of people who are helping me
prepare to celebrate Eucharist.

A Blessing for Beginnings

"I am the bread that gives life!
No one who comes to me will ever be hungry."

—John 6:35

Leader: Today we gather to continue your journey
of initiation as you prepare to receive
Communion for the first time.
We are ready to learn from one another
and from our Church community.
And so we pray:
God our Father, accept our thanks and praise
for your great love.
Jesus, Son of God, be with us in the Sacrament
of the Eucharist.
Holy Spirit, help us grow as members of the
Body of Christ.

Reader: *Read John 6:32–40.*
The word of the Lord.

All: **Thanks be to God.**

Leader: Let us ask God's blessing on our journey together.

All: **Holy Trinity, lead us to the table of the Eucharist.**
Teach us to love one another as you love us.
Help us be living signs of your presence in
the world,
and lead us to the fullness of your kingdom.
We pray in the words that Jesus taught us.
(Pray the Lord's Prayer.)

Leader: May the Lord be with us, now and always.

All: **Amen!**

Chapter 7

BELONGING

Your Life

To which team, group, or organization have you wanted to belong but were not invited or accepted? Use an initial, a word, or sketch a symbol to represent your answer.

Everyone needs to belong. When you belong, you share time and love with others. You help people, and they help you. Most young people know the feeling that comes from not belonging to a team or group that they really wanted to join.

You have a first name and a last name. Your first name reflects your individuality. You are different from your brother or sister. But your last name reflects the family of which you are a part.

It is the same way with your faith. You have your own individual way of praying and relating to God. You have your own faith questions and experiences. But you also have a faith "family" to whom you belong.

You are a member of the Catholic faith family. You became a member of this family when you were baptized. Through Baptism you became a follower of Jesus Christ. You became a Catholic **Christian** in the family of God.

We Are Invited : 71

In the Name of Jesus Christ

The following first-person account tells us how the Christian community got its start.

I remember that morning. I was in Jerusalem with my family for the Jewish feast of **Pentecost**. We saw a great crowd gathered. A man named Peter was speaking.

"Friends!" Peter said in a loud voice. You know that Jesus was a great teacher sent by God. Jesus died on a cross, but that was not the end of the story!"

"God set Jesus free from death," Peter
continued. "Jesus rose from the tomb, and
now he is with his Father in heaven. This very
day he sent the **Holy Spirit** to us as he had
promised. That promise is not just for us, his
friends. It is for you and your children, too!"

"What must we do?" my father called out.

"Turn to God, my friend," Peter answered.
"Be baptized in the name of Jesus Christ. Then
you will receive God's Holy Spirit, too."

That morning I was baptized with my
whole family. Now we all belong to the family
of Jesus Christ.

—based on Acts 2

Baptism and Confirmation

The Catholic Church welcomes new members through Baptism, Confirmation, and Eucharist. These sacraments are called **Sacraments of Initiation,** or "belonging."

We celebrate Baptism with water and holy words. All living things need water to stay alive. We need the water of Baptism to have new life forever with God.

The words of Baptism tell us that we belong to God. "I baptize you in the name of the Father, and of the Son, and of the Holy Spirit."

We celebrate Confirmation by being **anointed** with oil, a sign of our new holiness in Jesus, and by the laying on of hands. Oil is used to make the body strong. Confirmation helps us grow strong in our faith as we reach out to others who need God's love.

The words of Confirmation tell us that we have been given the Holy Spirit in a special way. "Be sealed with the Gift of the Holy Spirit."

You Ask

Why is Baptism the first sacrament?

Baptism makes us members of the Church and joins us to Jesus. In Baptism we first share in the **Paschal mystery** of Jesus' death and **resurrection**. All the other sacraments build on the grace of Baptism.
(See Catechism, #1213–1214)

Living Your Faith

Signed with the Cross

Write or draw three or four different ways you can be a sign of the cross for others.

Welcome

Reaching Out

Through baptism you belong to the family of God in a special way. You are called to welcome and include other people who want to be with you and your group of friends. Make a list of people to whom you can reach out and include in your activities. After each person's name, list a specific way you can include that person.

_____

_____

_____

_____

_____

_____

_____

_____

_____

_____

_____

Dear God—Father, Son, and Holy Spirit— thank you for calling me to belong to your family. Help me include others who want to belong in school, in church, and in life. Amen!

INVITED TO THE TABLE

Your Life

In writing recall a time when you were invited to a party that you really wanted to attend. There was probably food of some kind served at the party. What do you like best about sharing snacks or meals with friends?

_____

_____

_____

_____

_____

_____

_____

What if you went to a party and, when you arrived, the food was already gone. You would probably feel left out. Sharing a meal is a big part of any celebration. When you share food with others at a party or someone's home, including your own, you really feel that you belong.

Our Catholic family shares a very special meal, the **Eucharist.** During the Mass, we receive Jesus himself in the form of the sacred Bread and Wine. The altar is our family table.

You may have taken part in Mass before. But now you are getting ready to share completely in the celebration. You are invited to receive the spiritual food—the Body and Blood of Jesus in **Holy Communion.**

The Vine and the Branches

On the night before he died, Jesus went with his apostles to a garden to pray. The apostles were depressed and scared. They thought they would never see Jesus again. They wanted to stay close to him.

The apostles could have recalled a time when Jesus wanted to find a way to tell his friends they would never be separated from him. He looked at a beautiful grapevine growing along the garden wall. The grapevine gave Jesus an idea for a story.

"I am the vine, you are the branches. Whoever remains in me and I in him will bear much fruit, because without me you can do nothing.

"This is my commandment: love one another as I love you. No one has greater love than this, to lay down one's life for one's friends. You are my friends if you do what I command you.

"It was not you who chose me, but I who chose you and appointed you to go and bear fruit that will remain, so that whatever you ask the Father in my name he may give you."

—*John 15:5, 12–14, and 16*

Your Communion

As was said in the previous chapter, we become fully initiated into the Catholic Church through the Sacraments of Initiation. We are baptized. We are sealed with the Holy Spirit in Confirmation. We receive Jesus in Holy Communion. This is the way we accept Jesus' invitation to stay close to him.

The Sacraments of Initiation join us together with Jesus and with all his followers. Jesus is the head and all believers are the **Body of Christ.**

People of all ages celebrate the Sacraments of Initiation to become full members of the Church. Our Church invites adults and some children into the Body of Christ through the Rite of Christian Initiation of Adults. Other people are baptized as babies. Then, around the age of seven, they celebrate First Reconciliation and First Communion. They are confirmed some time later.

You Ask

How often should we receive Communion?

Baptism and Confirmation are once-in-a-lifetime celebrations. They mark us as God's own forever. But after we have received Communion for the first time, we are encouraged to come to the altar again and again throughout our lives as the Eucharist is the source and summit of the Christian life. Each time we celebrate the Eucharist at Mass, it is recommended that we receive Jesus in Communion if we are free of serious sin. (See Catechism, #1388)

Living Your Faith

My Response

When you receive an invitation, you have a responsibility to respond to it. Jesus invites you to grow closer to him by receiving Communion. Finish the following sentence in your own words about the response you want to make to Jesus' invitation. Sign your name.

Dear Jesus,

Thank you for inviting me to eat at your table. I want to receive you often. Here's what you can expect from me:

_____

_____

_____

_____

_____

_____

_____

_____

_____

Love,

_____

Responsibilities

List below other invitations you've accepted. Note what you will do about each one to show your responsibility and commitment to each.

_____
_____
_____
_____
_____
_____
_____
_____
_____
_____
_____
_____
_____

Dear God—Father, Son, and Holy Spirit—you have invited me to the table of the Eucharist. Help me stay committed to continually saying "yes" to your call. Amen!

GATHERING TO CELEBRATE

Your Life

Write about or draw a picture of a celebration you remember that made you feel really good inside. What does it take to have a good celebration?

It's no fun to celebrate alone. Good times are better when you share them with others. Family members, friends, and neighbors are part of your **community**, the group of people with whom you share special times.

As with other celebrations, we celebrate Eucharist with a group of people. Because the Eucharist is the heart and summit of the Church's life, we come together for Mass with members of our Church family, the **parish.**

Like a gathering for other celebrations, our gathering for Mass begins with greeting people. We share joy and faith through music and singing. We remember God's love, mercy, and forgiveness.

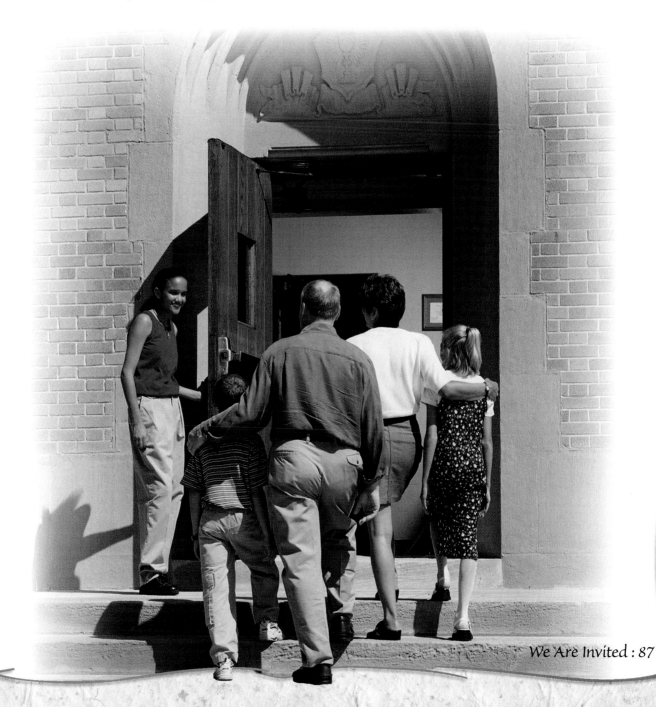

Like Family to One Another

The first Christians made the Eucharist the center of their lives.

They devoted themselves to the teaching of the apostles and to the communal life, to the breaking of the bread and to the prayers. Awe came upon everyone, and many wonders and signs were done through the apostles. All who believed were together and had all things in common; they would sell their property and possessions and divide them among all according to each one's need. Every day they devoted themselves to meeting together in the temple area and to breaking bread in their homes.

They ate their meals with exultation and sincerity of heart, praising God and enjoying favor with all the people. And every day the Lord added to their number those who were being saved.

—*based on Acts 2:42–47*

We Remember : 89

The Mass Begins

From the very beginning, it's easy to see that the Mass is a celebration. It often begins with an entrance hymn and procession. A hymn is a holy song. The procession is a special entrance of ministers who will help us celebrate.

The prayers and actions of the beginning of the Mass are called the **Introductory Rites.** The symbols given respect during the procession help us turn our hearts and minds to the great celebration of the Eucharist.

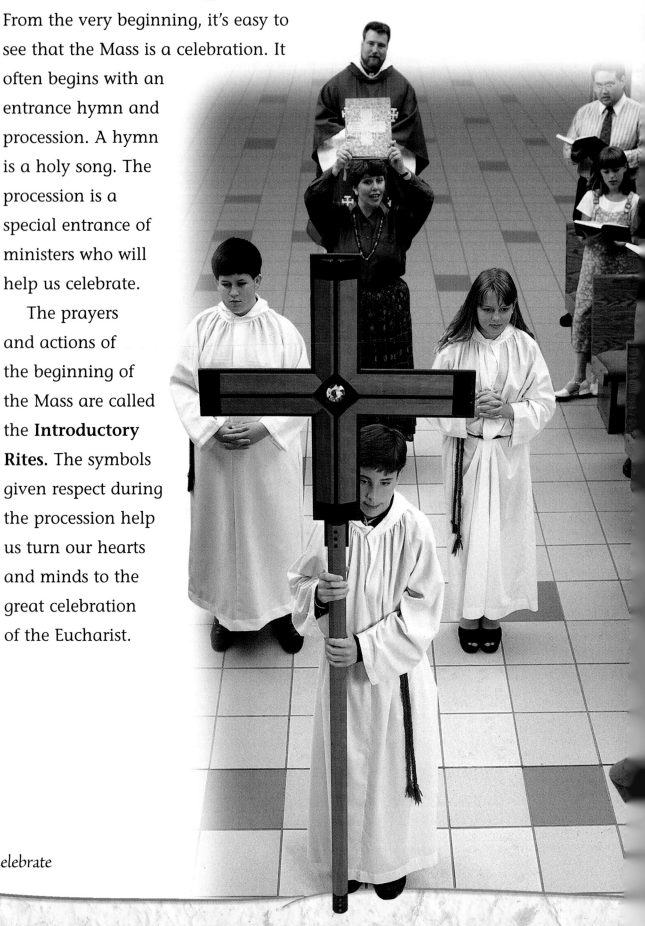

Jesus is really present in every part of the Mass. He is most truly with us in Communion, but he is also with us in the priest, the only person who can **preside** at, or lead, the Eucharist and consecrate the bread and the wine. Jesus is present in the other ministers. He is present in all of us gathered, the **assembly**, and in our activities.

At Mass we gather to celebrate the same Paschal mystery we celebrate in Baptism. We bless ourselves with water from the baptismal font or holy water font when we come into the church. The Mass begins with the Sign of the Cross, the same words with which we were baptized: "In the name of the Father, and of the Son, and of the Holy Spirit. Amen!"

You Ask

Why do we celebrate the Eucharist every week?

Gathering for Mass every week is how we show that we belong to the Body of Christ, for the Eucharist is the source and summit of the Christian life. We have a **duty**, or responsibility, to participate in the Mass once a week, on Sunday or on Saturday evening, and on holy days. The more we celebrate, the closer we come to Jesus and to one another.
(See Catechism, #2180–2182)

Living Your Faith

Celebrating the Mass

In the space below, draw symbols or write words that identify everything you like about going to Mass. (See if you can come up with five or more.)

HALLELUJAH

Celebrating Together

Think of other days or events your family celebrates. List below some of the ways you celebrate these special times together.

_____

_____

_____

_____

_____

_____

_____

_____

_____

_____

_____

_____

Dear God—Father, Son, and Holy Spirit—I join others as a member of your Catholic family at Mass. Help me celebrate also the other good things you give me every day. Amen!

FEASTING ON GOD'S WORD

our Life

Write down the topic of a funny family story you laugh at each time you hear it.

_____

_____

Write down the topic of a story about your friends that you love to tell.

_____

_____

Why do you like telling and hearing these stories?

_____

_____

_____

_____

Some stories are so good you want to hear them over and over. Good stories are like good news. They make you laugh or give you hope and nourish your spirit. Like a feast of good food, good stories can be shared with people you love.

Like most families, our Catholic family shares wonderful stories, too. At Mass we hear the good news of God's love in the words of the **Scriptures.** When we listen, it is as though God is speaking right to us. These Scripture stories nourish our spirit. Taking in God's word is part of the holy meal of the Eucharist.

Jesus, the Good Shepherd

Jesus knew that people needed to hear the good news of God's love. So one day Jesus compared himself to a shepherd, a person who cares for a flock of sheep. In Jesus' day almost everyone had seen shepherds at work in the fields.

"I am the good shepherd. A good shepherd lays down his life for the sheep. A hired man, who is not a shepherd and whose sheep are not his own, sees a wolf coming and leaves the sheep and runs away, and the wolf catches and scatters them. This is because he works for pay and has no concern for the sheep. I am the good shepherd and I know mine and mine know me, just as the Father knows me and I know the Father; and I will lay down my life for the sheep. I have other sheep that do not belong to this fold. These also I must lead, and they will hear my voice, and there will be one flock, one shepherd.

"This is why the Father loves me, because I lay down my life in order to take it up again. No one takes it from me, but I lay it down on my own. I have power to lay it down, and power to take it up again. This command I have received from my Father."

—*John 10:11–18*

Not everyone in the crowd understood Jesus' story, but some people did. It's the same way today when people hear Jesus' words from the Bible.

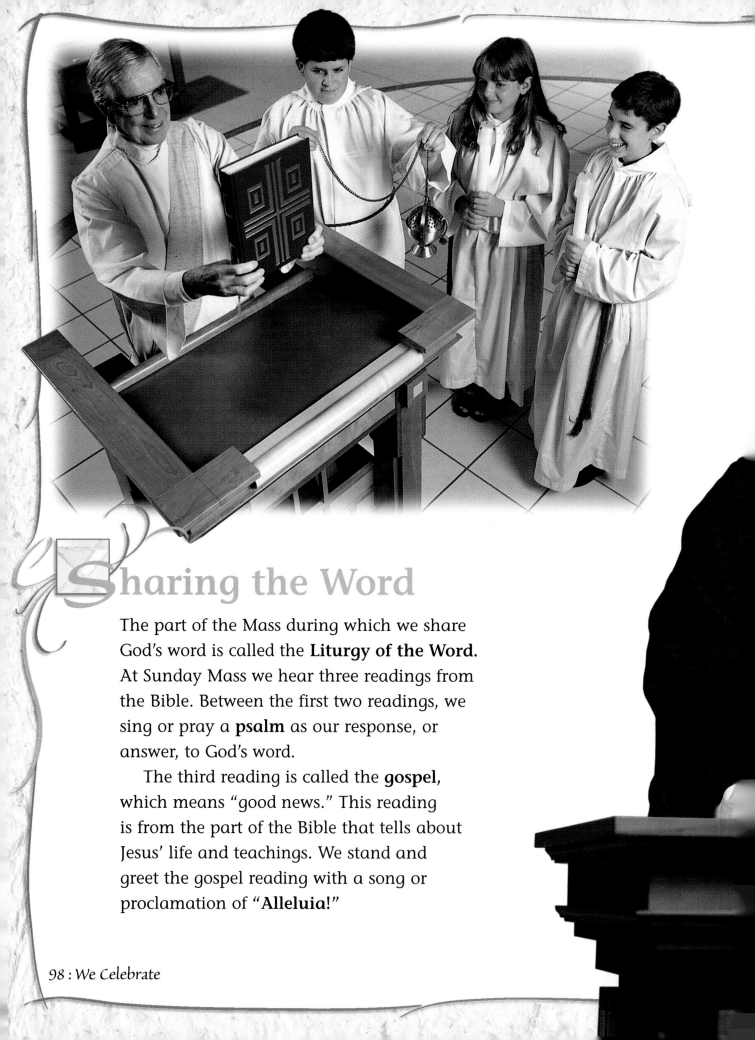

Sharing the Word

The part of the Mass during which we share God's word is called the **Liturgy of the Word.** At Sunday Mass we hear three readings from the Bible. Between the first two readings, we sing or pray a **psalm** as our response, or answer, to God's word.

The third reading is called the **gospel,** which means "good news." This reading is from the part of the Bible that tells about Jesus' life and teachings. We stand and greet the gospel reading with a song or proclamation of **"Alleluia!"**

After the readings the priest or deacon gives a **homily**, a short talk to help us understand and follow God's word. After the homily we stand and proudly state what we believe about our faith by praying the **Creed**.

We close the Liturgy of the Word by praying together for the needs of all people around the world. Nourishing our spirit on God's word makes us want to help nourish the spirit of others.

You Ask

How do we meet Jesus in God's word?

We believe that the Scriptures are God's own word, written down in human words. The good news of the Bible is the same good news that Jesus taught. One name for Jesus is "the Word of God." So when we share the word of God in the Scriptures, we are meeting Jesus, God's living Word. (See Catechism, #101–104)

 Living Your Faith

I Hear Good News

In the space below, draw a symbol or write about a Bible story that nourishes your spirit in a special way.

LUKE

Nourishment

The word of God found in the Scriptures is spiritual nourishment. After you are nourished, you are invited to be a source of nourishment for others. List below ways in which you can improve the way you nourish others.

In your family

_____

_____

_____

In school

_____

_____

_____

In the neighborhood

_____

_____

_____

Dear God—Father, Son, and Holy Spirit—your word is good news to me. It nourishes my spirit. Help me find ways to nourish the spirit of others. Amen!

CHAPTER 11
OFFERING OUR GIFTS

Your Life

List one or two of your family's favorite holidays and some of the food prepared or brought to the celebration. Then, next to each food, list who brought or who prepared the food.

Holiday	Food	Brought or made by
_____	_____	_____
_____	_____	_____
_____	_____	_____

What special food do you wish you could eat more often?

_____

_____

_____

You know that when people gather for a special occasion, they sometimes bring gifts of food. When we celebrate the Mass, we bring gifts of bread and wine to share. As Catholics, we believe that the bread and wine become Jesus' own Body and Blood. Jesus offers himself to the Father. This is the central act of our Catholic faith.

We share other things at Mass, too. We offer the gift of ourselves to God and to one another. We offer gifts of money to support the work of the parish and to help those who are in need.

The Wonderful Picnic

In the following story, a young boy tells how he offered all the gifts he had to give.

"Does anyone have any food to share?" That's what I heard the man named Philip ask. Thousands of people were sitting on the grass listening to Jesus teach. All the people shook their heads. No one had thought to bring food.

I took a deep breath. "Sir!" I called out. "I have five loaves of bread and a couple of fish."

The people around me laughed. Philip looked angry. "That's not enough food to feed even five people, never mind five thousand!" he said.

But I was looking at Jesus, who was smiling at me. He motioned for me to come forward. Jesus looked into my eyes and thanked me. Then he took the basket of food I held out to him.

Jesus took the bread in his hands and prayed the meal blessing. "Philip," he said, "you and the others pass this food to the people. Make sure everyone has enough to eat."

Something wonderful happened that day. From my five loaves and two fish, more than five thousand people had the best picnic ever. When the meal was finished, there were twelve baskets of leftovers!

"Thank you for sharing," Jesus said to me. And even Philip smiled.

—based on John 6:5–13

Our Offering to God

After the Introductory Rite and the Liturgy of the Word, we continue our celebration of the Mass with what is called the **Liturgy of the Eucharist.** During this part of the Mass, we offer our gifts and prayers to God the Father. Our greatest offering is Jesus, who offers himself to the Father by the power of the Holy Spirit. In the form of the sacred Bread and Wine, Jesus offers himself to us in Holy Communion.

At the **presentation of gifts**, members of the assembly bring the bread and wine to the priest. These gifts are placed on the **altar**, our table of offering. The priest blesses the bread and wine.

Along with the gifts of bread and wine, we offer gifts of money. This offering is called a **collection**. The money will help the parish community do its work and take care of those in need.

The money offering is also a sign that we offer ourselves to God. We are willing to share our time and our talents, as well as our treasure, with one another.

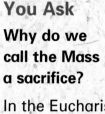

You Ask

Why do we call the Mass a sacrifice?

In the Eucharist we remember and celebrate Jesus' **sacrifice** for us on the cross. Jesus offered his life to his Father to save us from the power of sin and everlasting death. At every Mass, Jesus' sacrifice is made present. Every Mass is an offering for the sins of the living and the dead. We offer ourselves and our gifts, too. The whole Church joins with Jesus in the sacrifice of the Mass.
(See Catechism, #1366–1368)

Living Your Faith

Checking Yourself Out

Take a moment to check off any statement below that is true about you.

_____ I'm a very good listener.

_____ I can sense when someone else is having difficulties.

_____ My friends think I have a great sense of humor.

_____ People say that I'm reliable.

_____ I am honest.

_____ My family thinks I'm helpful.

_____ I speak up when someone is treated cruelly.

_____ I am willing to share my money with others.

_____ I am willing to give my time helping others.

_____ I am generous with giving others praise and compliments.

_____ I try not to judge others.

_____ I try not to be prejudiced against other people, races, or countries.

_____ I am coachable and willing to work together with others.

Now, list two statements from above that you did not check off.

_____

_____

What can you do to develop these qualities?

_____

_____

_____

_____

Gifts I Bring

In this chapter, we've looked at the gifts we bring to the Eucharistic table. Now go back to "Checking Yourself Out" on the previous page. Which of your gifts can you "bring to the table" in your interactions with family, friends, classmates, and parishioners? List them below.

_____

_____

_____

_____

_____

_____

_____

_____

_____

_____

Dear God—Father, Son, and Holy Spirit—you give me different talents. Help me share myself with others. Amen!

CHAPTER 12

REMEMBERING AND GIVING THANKS

Your Life

Everyone needs an imaginary memory box where you can store your strongest and favorite memories of great moments, good times, special feelings, and friendships. Such memories can be recalled whenever you need a lift, a laugh, or an assurance of being loved.

List words or initials for several of the treasured memories you store in your memory box.

_____

_____

_____

_____

_____

_____

_____

You know that every year families in our country share a special holiday centered around remembering the good things God has done for us. We call this holiday *Thanksgiving* because we give thanks to God for our families and our country. What things do you thank God for at Thanksgiving?

We give thanks to God at Mass, too. In fact, the word **Eucharist** means "thanksgiving." In the Eucharist we remember that God our Father sent Jesus to save us. We give thanks and lift our hearts to God in prayer.

Jesus Gives Thanks

On the night before he died, Jesus shared a special meal with his friends. They gathered to celebrate the **Passover**, a great Jewish holiday of thanksgiving.

Long ago God led the people of Israel out of the land of Egypt, where they had been slaves. He saved the people and set them free. Every year at the Passover meal, Jewish people remember God's saving love.

When the hour came, he took his place at table with the apostles. He said to them, "I have eagerly desired to eat this Passover with you before I suffer, for, I tell you, I shall not eat it [again] until there is fulfillment in the kingdom of God." Then he took a cup, gave thanks, and said, "Take this and share it among yourselves; for I tell you [that] from this time on I shall not drink of the fruit of the vine until the kingdom of God comes. Then he took the bread, said the blessing, broke it, and gave it to them, saying, "This is my body, which will be given for you; do this in memory of me." And likewise the cup after they had eaten, saying, "This cup is the new covenant in my blood, which will be shed for you."

—*Luke 22:14–20*

Our Great Thanksgiving Prayer

At Mass we do what Jesus did at his Last Supper with his friends. And we do remember him.

The most important prayer of the Mass is called the **Eucharistic Prayer.** It is our prayer of thanksgiving to God our Father.

During the Eucharistic prayer the priest repeats the words and actions of Jesus at the Last Supper. "This is my body," he says. "This is the cup of my blood."

Through the words of Christ and by the power of the Holy Spirit, the bread and wine truly become Jesus' Body and Blood. He is really with us in our thanksgiving meal, the Eucharist.

"Amen!" we pray. "Yes, we do believe!"

You Ask

Do the bread and wine really become Jesus' Body and Blood?

Yes. We believe that when the bread and wine are **consecrated** at Mass, they are no longer bread and wine. Jesus is truly and really present. We call this mystery **transubstantiation.** We don't fully understand how this great mystery of our faith happens. We believe and trust that Jesus is with us because he promised he would be. (See Catechism, #1333, 1376)

Living Your Faith

I Remember, I Give Thanks

In the space below, practice giving thanks by writing a personal thank you note to someone who helped you, loved you, or supported you through a tough time. Then copy what you've written onto a card or e-mail and send it to the person.

_____

_____

_____

_____

_____

_____

_____

_____

_____

_____

_____

_____

In Memory

Go back to your imaginary memory box and pull out a memory.
Make a note below as to how you can share your gratitude with
the person(s) involved in that memory, and then try to follow
through on the action.

_____

_____

_____

_____

_____

_____

_____

_____

_____

_____

Dear God—Father, Son, and Holy Spirit—I
remember how much you care for me. Help
me live with a grateful heart. Amen!

SHARING THE BREAD OF LIFE

Your Life

Circle two of the following things that you think you need the most in order to stay well and grow in maturity.

money	belonging	school
friends	achievement	athletics
love	safety	work
directions	adult friendship	family
peace	God	shelter
clothes	alertness	intelligence

Bread has always symbolized the basic food we need to sustain ourselves. As a figure of speech, the word *bread* has often also been used to symbolize the basic things that we need to sustain our spiritual and psychological needs as well.

The phrase "breaking bread" together is used to symbolize honest conversation and true friendship at a meal.

As Catholics, we "break bread" together at the Mass. God invites us to the table to share Jesus' own Body and Blood in Communion. Before we come to the table, we pray the **Lord's Prayer.** This is the prayer Jesus himself taught his followers. We pray, "Give us this day our daily bread and forgive us our trespasses."

To show that we are willing to forgive one another and make up, we exchange a **sign of peace.** Then the priest breaks the large Host as Jesus broke the sacred Bread at his Last Supper. We welcome Jesus as the **Lamb of God,** who takes away our sins and brings us peace.

The Bread That Gives Life

After Jesus had fed the crowd with only five loaves of bread and a few fish, people wanted him to perform more **miracles.**

So they said to him, "Sir, give us this bread always." Jesus said to them, "I am the bread of life. . . . Your ancestors ate

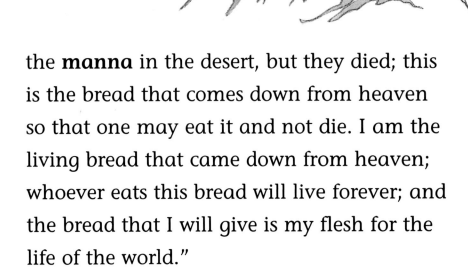

the **manna** in the desert, but they died; this is the bread that comes down from heaven so that one may eat it and not die. I am the living bread that came down from heaven; whoever eats this bread will live forever; and the bread that I will give is my flesh for the life of the world."

The Jews quarreled among themselves saying, "How can this man give us [his] flesh to eat?" Jesus said to them, "Amen, amen, I say to you, unless you eat the flesh of the Son of Man and drink his blood, you do not have life within you. Whoever eats my flesh and drinks my blood has eternal life, and I will raise him on the last day."

—*John 6:34–35, 49–54*

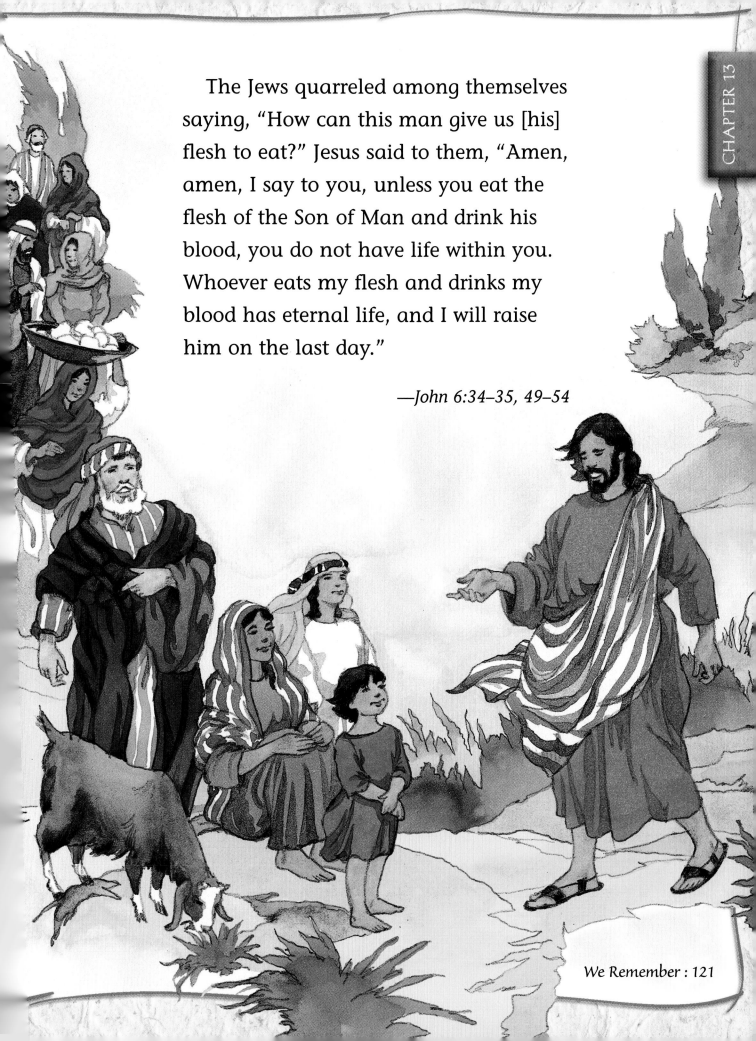

Holy Communion

When the time comes for Communion, the priest invites us to the table. "This is the Lamb of God, who takes away the sin of the world," he says, holding up the large Host. "Happy are we who are called to his supper!"

To receive Communion, we come forward in a procession and wait our turn prayerfully. We hold our hands up, cupping them with one hand on top of the other. The priest or **Eucharistic minister**, a person who helps the presider distribute the consecrated Hosts and the sacred Wine, holds up the Host and says, "The Body of Christ." We answer, "Amen!" and the Host is placed in our hands. Then we step aside and eat the sacred Bread.

A second option is to receive the Host on our tongue. After the priest or Eucharistic minister says, "The Body of Christ," we say, "Amen!" and then stick out our tongue and receive the Host.

On many Sundays we may also receive Communion from the cup. After swallowing the Host, we go to the deacon or Eucharistic minister who is holding the cup of consecrated Wine. The minister says, "The Blood of Christ." We answer, "Amen!" When we are offered the cup, we take a small sip.

Jesus is truly present in both forms of the Eucharist.

After receiving Communion, we return to our places. We can join in singing the Communion song or spend time in silent prayer.

You Ask

Who can receive Communion?

Baptized Catholics who have celebrated First Communion may receive Communion at Mass. A person who has committed mortal sin must receive **absolution** in the **Sacrament of Reconciliation** before receiving Communion. (See Catechism, #1384–1389)

Living Your Faith

"I Am the Bread of Life"

In the space below, write a paragraph explaining what you think Jesus meant by calling himself "The Bread of Life." It may help to remember the different things symbolized by bread that were talked about in this chapter.

_____

_____

_____

_____

_____

_____

_____

_____

_____

_____

_____

_____

_____

_____

Breaking Bread

In this chapter you have seen the sacred way we "break bread" during the Mass. You can also experience God's presence when you "break bread" with close friends and family. Plan for a time in the near future during which you can "break bread" with someone. On the lines below, outline who will be present and how you will carry out your plan.

_____

_____

_____

_____

_____

_____

_____

_____

_____

_____

_____

Dear God—Father, Son, and Holy Spirit—you feed us at the table of the Eucharist. Keep me close to you forever. Help me continue feeling your presence when I break bread with those I love. Amen!

CHAPTER 14

GOING FORTH TO LOVE AND SERVE

Your Life

Recall a time when, as a member of a team, organization, or performance group, you alone had to make the important play, decision, or action.

1) What was the situation?

_____

_____

_____

2) What did you need to do in order to make the important play or decision or to perform the action well?

_____

_____

_____

_____

Being part of a team, group, or community means that you will be depended upon to do your part to help the group meet its goals.

In unspoken ways, this means that you are trustworthy and responsible. Someone is counting on you. Without your support and participation, the job will not get done.

At the end of the Mass, each of us is sent to carry the message of God's love. We are sent to help carry out the work of Jesus in the world. Even the word **Mass** comes from a word that means "to be sent on a **mission**."

No one is too young or too old to be trusted with this mission. The Eucharist gives us what we need to bring good news to others. Receiving Jesus in Holy Communion strengthens us to love and serve others. We leave Mass with God's blessing to do this.

In the Breaking of the Bread

In the account below, we read about two followers of Jesus who share the good news of Jesus' resurrection.

It was the third day after Jesus died on the cross. Cleopas and I were sadly walking home from Jerusalem to our town, Emmaus. Then another traveler who we did not know joined us. He asked us why we were so sad.

Cleopas and I told the traveler all about Jesus. We talked about what a great teacher he was and how he fed us with Bread from heaven. We thought he was the **Messiah** sent by God to save us, but now he was dead.

The traveler shook his head. "Foolish people!" he said. "Don't you know that the Scriptures say the Messiah will give up his life for you?" And he explained God's word to us as we walked along.

We reached home as the sun was setting. "Stay and eat with us," Cleopas invited the traveler. "It's nearly night."

As we sat at the table, the traveler took the bread. He blessed it and broke it. And as he gave it to us, we suddenly understood. The traveler was Jesus whom God the Father had raised from death. In the blink of an eye, Jesus was gone. We ran all the way back to Jerusalem and burst into the room where Jesus' mother and his friends had gathered.

"Jesus is alive!" Peter said as he greeted us joyfully.

"We know!" I said. "He shared God's word with us as he walked with us on the road. And we recognized him in the breaking of the Bread."

—*based on Luke 24:13–35*

We Are Sent

Like Cleopas and his friend, it is in the breaking of the sacred Bread that we, too, meet Jesus. In the Eucharist, Jesus is present to us and shares God's word with us. Jesus offers his life to the Father by the power of the Holy Spirit. He comes to us in Communion.

And like those friends of Jesus, we want to share the joyful good news that Jesus is alive. At the end of the Mass, we are sent out to serve others. "Go in peace to love and serve the Lord," the priest or deacon says. "Thanks be to God!" we all answer together.

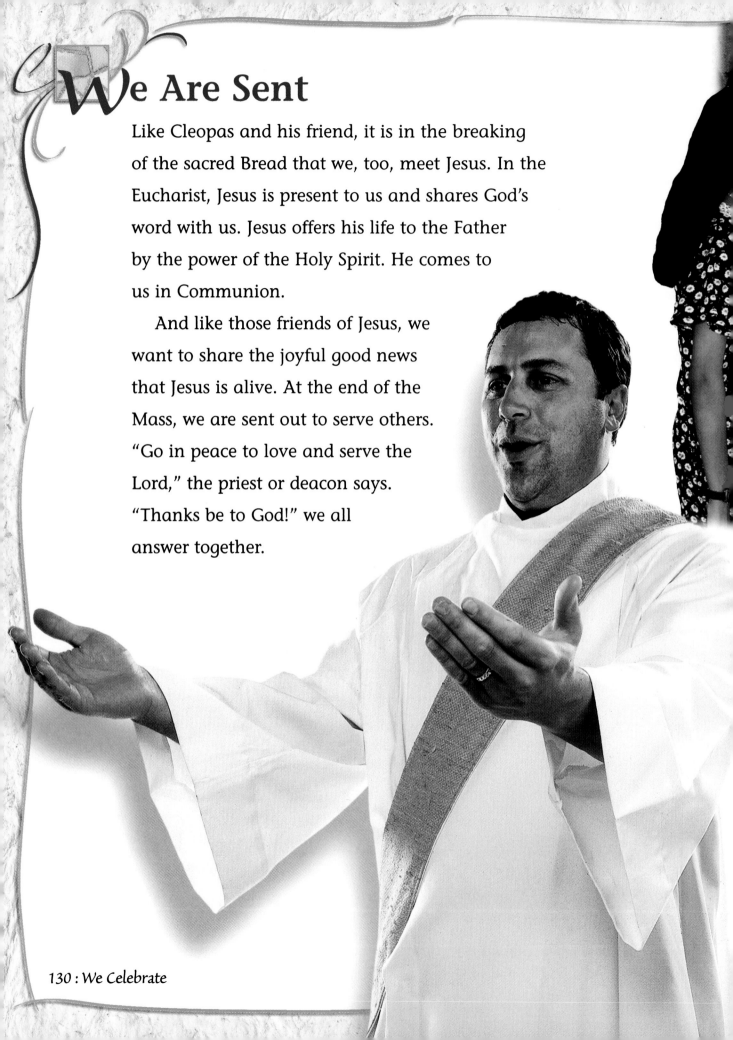

You Ask

How is the Eucharist a sign of God's kingdom?

Jesus came to announce God's kingdom of justice, love, and peace. That kingdom is both here in our midst and yet to come in fullness. In the Eucharist we receive a taste of the heavenly banquet we will share with all faithful people in the fullness of God's kingdom. Strengthened by the Eucharist, we work to bring justice, love, and peace to everyone. *(See Catechism, #1402–1405)*

When we leave the church after Mass, we should be different from when we came in. The Eucharist can change us. It can bring us closer to God and to others. The Eucharist takes away our less serious sins. It can help us make peace with everyone.

In the Eucharist we become one body, just as many grains of wheat make one loaf of bread. When we go out into the world, we should recognize Jesus in everyone. The simple truth Jesus taught us is that when we love and serve Jesus, we love and serve one another.

Living Your Faith

Loving and Serving

Draw or write three things you will do to share God's love with others.

What Can I Do?

"Let no one have contempt for your youth, but set an example for those who believe, in speech, conduct, love, faith, and purity" (1 Timothy 4: 12).

In this time of sacramental preparation, you have seen that as a Catholic:

You have been included—now go and include others.

You have been invited—now go and invite others.

You are part of the celebration—now go and celebrate the many good things God has given you.

You are spiritually nourished—now go and nourish the spirits of others.

You are given the bread of life—now go and break bread with friends and loved ones.

You remember Jesus' sacrifice and teachings—now go, notice, and remember God's moments of grace.

You are called and sent—now go and deliver the gift of your faith and abilities where needed.

Summarize what "living the Eucharist" now means to you.

_____

_____

_____

_____

_____

Dear God—Father, Son, and Holy Spirit—thank you for coming to us in the Eucharist. Help me live the Eucharist out in the world. Amen!

Catholic Prayers

The Sign of the Cross

In the name of the Father,
and of the Son,
and of the Holy Spirit.
Amen.

The Lord's Prayer

Our Father, who art in heaven,
hallowed be thy name;
thy kingdom come;
thy will be done on earth as it is in heaven.
Give us this day our daily bread;
and forgive us our trespasses
as we forgive those who trespass against us;
and lead us not into temptation,
but deliver us from evil.
Amen.

Hail Mary

Hail, Mary, full of grace,
the Lord is with you!
Blessed are you among women,
and blessed is the fruit of your womb, Jesus.
Holy Mary, Mother of God,
pray for us sinners,
now and at the hour of our death.
Amen.

Glory to the Father (Doxology)

Glory to the Father,
and to the Son,
and to the Holy Spirit,
as it was in the beginning,
is now, and will be for ever.
Amen.

Blessing Before First Communion

May the Lord Jesus touch your ears to receive his word,
and your mouth to proclaim his faith.
May you come with joy to his supper
to the praise and glory of God.
Amen.

Prayer Before Communion

How holy is this feast
in which Christ is our food:
his passion is recalled,
grace fills our hearts,
and we receive a pledge of the glory to come.

—based on a prayer of Thomas Aquinas

Thanksgiving After Communion

Lord our God,
we honor the memory of Saint Pius X
and all your saints
by sharing the bread of heaven.
May it strengthen our faith
and unite us in your love.
We ask this in the name of Jesus the Lord.
Amen.

Order of the Mass

Introductory Rites

- **Entrance Song**   We sing a hymn or psalm as the priest and other ministers come to the altar.

- **Greeting**   The priest, the only person who can preside at the Eucharist, begins by praying the Sign of the Cross. The people answer, "Amen."

- **Rite of Blessing and Sprinkling with Holy Water or Penitential Rite**   Sometimes the assembly is blessed with holy water. Sometimes the priest asks us to recall our sins and ask for God's mercy by saying, "Lord, have mercy; Christ, have mercy; Lord, have mercy."

- **Glory to God**   We sing or pray this prayer of praise.

- **Opening Prayer**   We prepare ourselves to hear God's word. The priest says, "Let us pray . . ." The people answer, "Amen."

Liturgy of the Word

- **First Reading**   This reading is usually taken from the Old Testament. The stories tell about things that happened before Jesus was born. The lector ends by saying, "The word of the Lord." The people answer, "Thanks be to God."

- **Responsorial Psalm**   This is a prayer taken from the Book of Psalms. The people repeat the response after each verse.

- **Second Reading**   This reading is taken from the New Testament letters. The letters tell about the actions of the first Christians. The lector says, "The word of the Lord." The people respond, "Thanks be to God."

- **Gospel Acclamation (Alleluia)**   We stand and greet the good news with a word that means "Praise God!"

- **Gospel**   The deacon or priest reads from the New Testament books that tell the story of Jesus' life and teachings. Before beginning the reading, the deacon or priest says, "The Lord be with you." The people say, "And also with you." The deacon or priest says, "A reading from the holy gospel according to (name)." The people respond, "Glory to you, Lord." After the reading of the gospel, the deacon or priest says, "The gospel of the Lord" and the people say, "Praise to you, Lord Jesus Christ."

- **Homily**   The priest or deacon explains the meaning of God's word for us today.

- **Profession of Faith (Creed)**   We stand and proclaim what we believe.

- **General Intercessions**   We pray for the needs of all people. The deacon or lector reads the intercessions, each of which ends with "We pray to the Lord." The people answer after each intercession, "Lord, hear our prayer."

Liturgy of the Eucharist

- **Offertory Song (Presentation of Gifts)**   We present gifts of bread, wine, and ourselves that we will offer to God. Money is collected to be used for the needs of the Church. We sing a hymn of offering.

- **Preparation of the Bread and Wine**   We thank God for the gifts of bread and wine. The priest says, "Blessed are you, Lord, God of all creation . . ." The people answer, "Blessed be God for ever."

- **Prayer over the Gifts**   The priest asks God to bless and accept our gifts. The priest says, "Pray, my brothers and sisters, that our sacrifice may be acceptable to God, the almighty Father." The people respond, "May the Lord accept the sacrifice at your hands for the praise and glory of his name, for our good, and the good for all his Church."

- **Preface**   The priest begins the Eucharistic Prayer by recalling, in the presence of the assembly, God's wonderful kindness.

- **Acclamation (Holy, Holy, Holy Lord)**   The people join together in singing or praying this response to the preface.

- **Eucharistic Prayer**   The Eucharistic Prayer is our great prayer of thanksgiving. The priest prays in our name. He asks the Holy Spirit to bless our gifts and us. He uses the words of Jesus at the Last Supper to consecrate the bread and wine. They become the Body and Blood of Jesus.

- **Memorial Acclamation**   We proclaim our belief that Jesus is truly present. There are several forms of the memorial acclamation.

- **Great Amen**   The priest brings the Eucharistic Prayer to a close by singing or saying, "Through him, with him, in the unity of the Holy Spirit, all glory and honor is yours, almighty Father, for ever and ever." The people sing or say, "Amen." We join ourselves with Jesus' gift of himself to the Father by the power of the Holy Spirit.

Communion Rite

- **Lord's Prayer** We pray the words Jesus taught us.

- **Sign of Peace** We exchange a handshake of peace with those around us.

- **Breaking of the Bread** The priest breaks off a small piece of the consecrated Host and places it in the chalice. This shows that all Masses are one. The consecrated Host is divided into parts, which shows that we all share in the one Body of Christ.

- **Lamb of God** The people sing or say a song of praise to Jesus, the Lamb of God.

- **Prayers before Communion** The priest genuflects and holds up the consecrated Host. He says, "This is the Lamb of God who takes away the sins of the world. Happy are those who are called to his supper." The people respond, "Lord, I am not worthy to receive you, but only say the word and I shall be healed."

- **Holy Communion** We receive the Body and Blood of Jesus in Holy Communion. The priest or Eucharistic minister says, "The Body of Christ." The person receiving the sacred Bread says, "Amen." The priest or Eucharistic minister says, "The Blood of Christ." The person receiving the sacred Wine says, "Amen."

- **Communion Song or Silent Reflection** A song or prayer of thanksgiving is offered.

- **Prayer after Communion** The priest, speaking for us, thanks God for sharing Jesus with us.

Concluding Rite

- **Greeting** The priest says, "The Lord be with you." The people answer, "And also with you."

- **Blessing** We make the Sign of the Cross as the priest asks God's blessing on us. The people answer, "Amen."

- **Dismissal** We are sent forth to carry on the work of Jesus. The priest says, "Go in peace to love and serve the Lord." The people answer, "Thanks be to God."

Holy Communion

Rules and Practices

Catholics follow these rules and practices to show respect for the Eucharist:

- To receive Holy Communion, we must be free from mortal sin. When we have contrition, receiving Holy Communion frees us from venial sin.

- To honor the Lord, we fast for one hour before receiving Communion. We go without food or drink, except water or medicine.

- Catholics are required to receive Holy Communion at least once a year, if possible during Easter time. But we are encouraged to receive Communion every time we participate in the Mass.

- Catholics are permitted to receive Communion at a second Mass on the same day.

How to Receive Communion

When we receive Jesus in Holy Communion, we welcome him with our whole bodies, minds, and spirits.

Here are steps to follow when you receive Communion:

- Fold your hands, and join in singing the Communion hymn as you walk to the altar.

- When it is your turn, you can receive the consecrated Host in your hand or on your tongue. To receive it in your hand, hold your hands out with the palms up. Place one hand underneath the other, and cup your hands slightly. To receive the Host on your tongue, fold your hands, and open your mouth, putting your tongue out.

- The priest or Eucharistic minister says, "The Body of Christ," and you answer, "Amen." The priest or minister places the Host in your hand or on your tongue.

- Step aside and stop. If you have received the Host in your hand, carefully take it from your palm, and put it in your mouth. Chew and swallow the Host.

- You may also be offered Communion from the cup. After swallowing the Host, walk to where the cup is offered. The deacon or Eucharistic minister says, "The Blood of Christ." You answer, "Amen."

- Take the cup from the priest, deacon, or minister. Take a small sip, and carefully hand the cup back.

- Quietly return to your place. Pray a prayer of thanksgiving.

Illustrated Glossary of the Mass

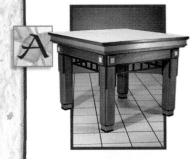

altar

('ôl•tər): The table of the Eucharist. At the altar the sacrifice of the Mass is offered to God.

ambo

('am•bō): The lectern, or reading stand, from which the Scriptures are proclaimed. The ambo is sometimes called "the table of the word."

assembly

(ə•'sem•blē): The community gathered to celebrate the Eucharist or another sacramental liturgy.

baptismal font

('bap•tiz•məl fânt): The bowl-shaped container or pool of water used for Baptism. The word *font* means "fountain."

Book of the Gospels

('bùk 'əv 'thə 'gäs•pəls): A decorated book containing the readings from the four Gospels used during the Liturgy of the Word.

cantor

('kan•tər): The minister who leads the singing at Mass and during other Church celebrations.

chalice

('cha•ləs): The special cup used at Mass to hold the wine that becomes the Blood of Christ.

ciborium

(sə•'bōr•ē•əm): A container for hosts. A ciborium may hold the smaller consecrated Hosts used for Communion. A covered ciborium also holds the Blessed Sacrament in the tabernacle.

cruets

('krü•əts): Small pitchers or containers for the water and wine used at Mass. Many parishes use larger pitchers to hold the wine, especially if people will be receiving Communion from the cup.

deacon

('dē•kən): A man who is ordained to serve the Church by baptizing, proclaiming the gospel, preaching, assisting the priest at Mass, witnessing marriages, and doing works of charity.

Eucharist

('yü•k(ə)rəst): The sacrament of Jesus' presence under the form of sacred Bread and Wine. We receive Jesus' own Body and Blood as Holy Communion during the Eucharistic celebration, the Mass. The word *Eucharist* means "thanksgiving."

host

('hōst): A round piece of unleavened bread used at Mass. When the host is consecrated, it becomes the Body and Blood of Christ. We receive the consecrated Host in Holy Communion.

incense

(in•sen(t)s): Materials made from oils and spices that are burned to make sweet-smelling smoke. At Mass and in other liturgical celebrations, incense is sometimes used to show honor for holy things and as a sign of our prayers rising to God.

Lectionary

('lek•shə•ner•ē): The book of the Scripture readings used at Mass.

lector

('lek•tər): A minister who proclaims God's word at Mass or during other liturgical celebrations. The word *lector* means "reader."

offering

('ȯ•f(ə)r•riŋ): The gifts we give at Mass. Members of the assembly bring our offering of bread and wine to the altar. We also give an offering of money, called a *collection,* to support the work of the Church. The highest offering is Jesus himself, who offers himself to the Father in the Eucharistic Prayer.

paten

('pa•tən): The plate or dish used at Mass to hold the bread that will become the Body and Blood of Christ.

priest

('prēst): A man who is ordained to serve God and the Church by celebrating the sacraments, preaching, and presiding at Mass.

Sacramentary

('sa•krə•'men•'ter•ē): The book of prayers used by the priest at Mass. Another name for this book is the **missal** ('mi•səl). Members of the assembly may use booklets called **missalettes** ('mi•səl•'ets) to follow the readings and join in the responses and prayers.

sanctuary

('saŋ(k)•chə•wer•ē): The part of the church where the altar and the ambo are located. The word *sanctuary* means "holy place."

server
('sər•vər): A minister, usually a young person, who helps the priest and deacon at Mass. A person who carries out this ministry is known as an **acolyte** ('a•kə•'līt).

tabernacle
('ta•bər•na•kəl): The box, chest, or container in which the Blessed Sacrament is reserved, or kept. The tabernacle may be placed in the sanctuary or in a special Eucharistic chapel or area. A lamp or candle is kept burning near the tabernacle as a sign that Jesus is present. The word *tabernacle* means "meeting place."

usher
('ə•sh ər): A minister of hospitality who welcomes members of the assembly to Mass and helps direct processions and collections.

vestments
('ves(t)•mənts): The special clothing worn by the priest and some other ministers for Mass and other liturgical celebrations. The priest wears an **alb** ('alb), **chasuble** ('chaz(h)•ə•bəl), and **stole** ('stōl). The deacon wears a **dalmatic** (dal•'mat•ik) or an alb and a stole. The colors of vestments usually indicate the season of the liturgical year.

wine
(wīn): A drink made from fermented juice from grapes. At Mass the consecrated Wine becomes the Body and Blood of Christ. We may receive the consecrated Wine from the cup at Communion.